1

GOD IS IN BUSINESS

It was a beautiful evening early in May, the sort that invites even the most reluctant gardener to pick up a spade and fork. Ken's wife, Becky, had been nattering to him about the bedding plants she'd bought to plant out in the patch overlooked by their bedroom. There was just one problem, namely an assortment of buttercups, dandelions and plantains that she'd begged him to dig out. Realising he'd run out of excuses, he'd sprinkled on fertiliser, turned the soil over and had removed the weeds. The patch was now prepared. It was time to park his fork and spade back in the shed.

Even Harry, who lived alone in the next house down from Ken, was tempted out into the sunshine, attracted more by the prospect of a chat than by improving his garden. Weeds flourished in his borders, although a few perennials lived on as a reminder of earlier days when it all looked much tidier. Ken suspected Harry had a bee in his bonnet or, rather, under his trusty flat cap, and soon found he wasn't mistaken.

"...and she can't see it as our problem, the miserable old bat!" complained Harry. "Yes, I know it's my tree, but it's her wall. I've checked. I never planted that tree; it planted itself. Now she's telling me I'll be liable for rebuilding her wall and for any damage to her plants and shrubs. Summat about 'I'm not interested in the garden like them that lived here before'. She says I should've sorted it five years ago..."

"D'you want to show me?" asked Ken.

Yes, indeed, it was a very messy situation. Towards the back of Harry's garden, a healthy sycamore tree had grown to fifteen feet tall. Its trunk was only about a foot inside the wall on Harry's side. A ten-foot section of the wall between his garden and Florence's was about to collapse, pushed over by the tree. It seemed harsh on Harry, *but*, thought Ken to himself, *Florence is right: if he'd only acted at the proper time...*

Ken hadn't ever talked with Harry about money but was pretty sure he'd be hard pushed to pay a tradesman to resolve the problems. Was this, at least in part, why he was so 'wound up'?

"Tell you what," piped up Ken, "why don't we pray about it? That's what me and Becky do when we feel we're stuck."

"You what?" retorted Harry. "I know you go to church and all that, but surely God-if-he's-there can't be interested in silly little things like my tree and her wall? I'd have thought he'd have much more important stuff to do. Wars to stop. Starving people to feed. Galaxies to create. I couldn't bother him over such trivial stuff!"

"Hmm...well, Becky and I do," replied Ken. "The God we believe in isn't limited by 'space-time' like we are. All through the Bible, we can read about God changing circumstances both for big and little things. Freedom from slavery. Food for hungry people in the desert. Making a borrowed axe head float that fell into a river. Coming to the rescue when they ran out of wine at a wedding. Helping fisherman to a bumper catch...

There's lots and lots, and I know Jesus gets excited when we ask him to get involved. Yes, he may have created the universe, but I believe that dealing with us is what he enjoys the most. When he was here on earth, Jesus never walked past anybody who was in trouble and asked for his help… and it's just the same today…"

Harry could see Ken was now in full flow. He raised his hand as if to say, "Stop there!" and, with an air of resignation, asked his neighbour to get on with it, whatever 'it' was.

"Lord Jesus Christ," prayed Ken, "we invite you to come right into the middle of this thorny situation between Harry and Florence. We trust you to bring peace between them, and to help us find a creative way of sorting it out. Amen."

2

SOMETHING WENT WRONG

April had been unseasonably warm and sunny, with the showers arriving in May. The next morning and afternoon were wet, but by six o'clock the clouds had cleared away to reveal yet another bright and cheerful evening. The energetic Becky placed a fruit cake in the oven to bake, then extracted a reluctant Ken from his armchair to help put in her bedding plants. It would only take half an hour, she insisted. Ken just managed to stop her wading into the soft, freshly dug soil in her wellies and persuaded her that they needed to place planks to form walkways between the rows. He left her stamping her feet with irritation whilst he toddled off to the shed to find some timber. Finally, they got down to work, and within an hour they'd laid out several neat rows with a diamond shape in the middle. And then they became aware of Harry's gaze, admiring their team effort.

Unfortunately, Harry's neighbourhood problem was still bugging him.

"I just can't understand what makes some folk so mean and spiteful, like" – and he drew a breath, turned his head and pointed with his thumb – "*her*. I mean, nearly everybody else on our road's a decent neighbour. I'm just unlucky to live next door to the bad one!"

Becky had a talent for telling home truths without causing offence, and asked with seeming innocence, "Harry, what d'you think Florence would say about you if we asked her?"

Shuffling awkwardly, Harry went quiet, as if inspecting his boots.

"I think you're describing what's wrong with the world," said Ken. "I'm guilty too, Harry. Sometimes I get in a bad mood, especially if I don't get my own way."

Becky nodded knowingly, before disappearing indoors to inspect her cake.

"Sometimes I pick quarrels. I judge people rather than trying to understand them. Sometimes it's a shock to find out how prejudiced I am. We can laugh about it when it's me losing my rag with Becky," continued Ken, "but you can see the same patterns being worked out in the way world leaders behave. And, if you take it further, the results are wars, terror, people smuggling, greed by bankers, slavery…"

"Aw, maybe so," replied Harry, "but that's just the way of the world, isn't it?"

"It's not how God designed it," answered Ken. "His idea was for men and women to enjoy his company and let him guide us through our lives. But we – men and women – decided it would be better for us to go our own way and to shut him out. And that's where the problem lies: a great big gulf between us and God."

"Yes, but you aren't telling me God doesn't make allowances for us?" asked Harry. "I mean, most of us do our best to live as good people. We don't deliberately mess things up."

"Talk about messing things up!" cried a tearful Becky, charging down the garden path. "Look at this!

It's my own stupid fault for trying to do too many things at once!"

As her voice tailed off, Ken and Harry looked at one very flat cake. Becky never used self-raising flour; she used plain flour and added the baking powder separately. Except that this time, she'd forgotten it. There was nothing she could do but to start over again. All those lovely cherries, nuts and sultanas, destined for the recycle bin…

As Ken placed his arm around her shoulder, he turned to Harry and said, "It's like the position God was in with us and the world. People had messed it up so badly, it looked like he'd have to start all over again, unless he could find a rescue plan."

Then he turned and walked indoors with Becky. He left her to choose a TV programme whilst he washed up the baking tins and mixer.

3

AMAZING GRACE

"Well, I'm glad somebody likes my first effort!" laughed Becky as she watched the bluetits pecking away at the bird feeder where her baking had been crumbled up. She and Ken were sprawled out on wicker chairs, in front of a patio table with coffee cups and a plate holding her new fruit cake, which this time contained baking powder. Ken took a forkful, tasted it, closed his eyes and licked his lips with delight.

Harry, who must have caught a whiff of the coffee, stepped up to the garden wall. It was difficult to make out his mood – as if he was pleased yet puzzled. Becky cut him a slice.

"Well, you'll never guess what happened last night," he began. "She might be an old cow, but her nephew Jack's alright. He came to visit her yesterday and came to see me about the wall. And – you won't believe this – he's a tree surgeon. He says he'll take the tree out, then get his mates to help rebuild our garden wall in his spare time, all for free…"

"Harry, that's brilliant news!" said Ken. "So – no more worrying about it, and no more arguments with Florence?"

But Harry's expression told Ken he'd jumped the gun. "Thing is, I don't feel right accepting charity," he explained. "I feel like I ought to pay him, but I haven't got anything like enough."

Becky furrowed her brow in a knowing sort of way. "Harry, am I right that Ken prayed about the problem with you? D'you think something's happened 'cause of that?"

"Bit of an interesting coincidence, yeah, I'll give you that," he replied.

Ken took up the theme. "Harry, do you remember we were talking about the way people had messed up God's world, and how God needed a rescue plan? I think what's happened is just like that. You couldn't sort out the tree and the wall by your own efforts. You couldn't pay for it to be done. Now Jack's offering to sort it for you, and all you can do is say 'yes, please' and 'thank you'.

"God had an answer, too. He sent his son, Jesus, to live on earth with us. Jesus showed us what it's like to live God's way in a broken world. And – can you believe it? – we killed him! But, in his dying, God made a way for men and women to be forgiven and to become new people, to live like he first intended."

Seeing Ken was in danger of losing Harry's attention, Becky dived in. "It's a free gift, Harry! We couldn't mend ourselves any more than you could get your wall mended. Jesus died to buy our forgiveness and it's there for the taking, just like you simply need to say yes to Jack's offer."

Harry looked confused and went into boot inspection mode. "It sort of goes against the grain," he said. "Something for nothing doesn't add up."

"Well... it's not *quite* something for nothing," said a thoughtful Ken. "Jack's made you an offer with no strings attached. But if you accept it, you'll find it'll change the way you treat Florence. That'll be part of your 'thank you'."

"And," added Becky, "it's like that with God's free gift, Harry. If you thank Jesus for dying on the cross for you, it changes the way you live. You can't carry on living just to please yourself. Ken and I find we want to please God. And the best way to do that is to let him share our lives and to join in with his adventure."

A thoughtful Harry placed his plate back on the table. "A very nice piece of cake, thank you very much," he said. Then he turned around and disappeared indoors.

4

A NEW CREATION

It was the skip, the pallets of building stones and the sand outside Florence's that first alerted Ken and Becky that something was afoot. It was Friday afternoon, and they'd just returned after spending half term week at a cottage in North Wales with their daughter, her husband and three small children. A change, if not a rest... As they parked their suitcases in the bedroom, they looked over at Harry's garden and, sure enough, saw the tree had disappeared. They turned to face each other, then Becky exclaimed:

"Yippee! He's said yes!"

The following afternoon, three strapping men arrived in a van, equipped with shovels, picks, bags of cement, pebbles, planks and a mixer. At teatime on Sunday, when the van pulled away, Ken and Becky couldn't resist walking down the road from where they could glimpse the beginnings of the wall, set into freshly laid concrete. How much lighter Florence's garden looked! The following Saturday, the men returned to

complete the wall, and on the Sunday, they returned the soil from two large mounds into the gaps that remained on either side.

The following day, Ken was just putting away his lawnmower when he noticed Harry ambling up towards the garden wall. Ken began:

"Well, now, what a tidy job they've made! I bet you're pleased you said yes to Jack's offer!"

"Yeah," replied Harry, "I thought about what you and Becky said. You're right; I'd have been daft not to accept his help."

Ken decided to 'push the boat out'. He asked, "How about the other offer, Harry? Have you thought any more about accepting God's offer of Jesus' free gift?" Harry coughed awkwardly and, as was his habit, looked down at his feet. So, Ken continued:

"There's another way God's and Jack's offers are alike. His wall's not a patched-up version of the old one, although it reuses the materials from it. It's a brand-new wall built on solid foundations. Those of us who follow Jesus find our lives are like this. I don't like to sound like a walking bible but here's one of my favourite verses from St Paul: 'If anyone is in Christ, the new creation has come. The old has gone, the new is here!'"[1]

Ken decided to ignore Harry's rolling of his eyes. "Becky and I are aware of Jesus gradually changing our attitudes. She's much more grateful and thankful for things. She says I'm learning to get less impatient. And I'm finding I have more courage. At work last week, I prayed for a friend's swollen knee to get better. And then I stuck up for one of my colleagues even though we don't get on, because he was being unfairly treated. And this week…"

"Ken, I'll have to stop you there," said Harry, raising his hand. "I'm glad for you that you're enjoying your religion. There's just one problem when you talk about Jesus. People don't rise from the dead. Let's face it, Ken, you're praying to a corpse. And I can't see any

---

[1] 2 Corinthians 5:17

evidence that this God you talk about does anything at all nowadays. Are you sure he's really there?"

And with those words, Harry turned his back, then shuffled back indoors leaving Ken with his mouth gaping wide open. What sort of an answer could he give?

The following Sunday, Ken asked to speak to his vicar. They talked and prayed for a few minutes, then later that day an envelope containing two books arrived on his doorstep.

5

THE UNBELIEVABLE TRUTH

"So," asked Ken as he took a sip of ale, "we're agreed Jesus lived on earth; we agree he died on a cross; and we agree his disciples started the church?"

Harry nodded. Ken had offered to buy him a drink at the pub or the coffee shop on Saturday morning, saying Harry had thrown him such a big challenge that he had to reply. Harry had chosen his local, but at a time when he knew they could find a quiet corner.

"What I can't understand" said Ken, "is how the disciples came to start the church if their leader was dead. In the Gospel accounts, they thought they'd been mistaken in recognising him as God's son, and they were frightened and confused. How come they suddenly became so courageous and bold?"

"Yes, but those stories are all you've got to go on," replied Harry, "and then the tales of the resurrection contradict each other. They'll have been told and re-told so many times, like Chinese whispers…"

"Hold on!" countered Ken, grateful he'd done his homework. "You may be right that the details differ between the accounts, but all of them are clear that Jesus rose from the dead and appeared to his disciples. All of them tell you the disciples were taken by surprise, even scared out of their wits. I'd have been more worried if all the accounts *did* completely agree. It would mean they weren't independent." Ken began to explain why he believed the stories had been written within the lifetime of the first disciples, but it was clear Harry wasn't too bothered about this.

The argument swung to and fro, exploring the details of who saw Jesus when and where. At last Ken took a swig of his beer, then asked, "Come on then, Harry. Tell me your theory about what happened to Jesus' body."

"Obviously," said Harry, "somebody took it away."

"But who?" asked Ken. "Not the religious leaders, nor the Romans. Both of these wanted the 'Jesus' movement to be snuffed out before it became troublesome. If they had the body, why didn't they just produce it for all to see? The obvious choice would have been the disciples. But how could they possibly have become bold, fearless men willing to risk their lives and be martyred, if they knew they were living a lie, telling everyone Jesus was alive when they knew he wasn't?"

Harry challenged Ken, asking, "How do we know they were martyrs? Again, you've only got the Bible to go on."

But then Ken mentioned the writings of Josephus and of Pliny the Younger, a Roman governor who was finding the Christians a troublesome, bold and passionate group who wouldn't recognise the emperor as their ultimate authority. In 112 AD he wrote to emperor Trajan asking for advice on how to deal with them.

Halfway down their second pint, Ken turned to Harry and said, "I rest my case. And I bet you, Harry, that if you read the accounts for yourself, you'll come to the same conclusion as me and Becky; they have a ring of truth about them."

Ken sat back, relaxed and sipped his beer. Harry, too, took a break from their discussion. They talked about football, TV comedies and Harry's ex-wife, until Ken's mobile pinged to ask him what he wanted for lunch. Just as they reached home, they parted ways, at which point Harry said:

"Look, Ken, I don't know what the explanation is. But there'll be some way of explaining what happened to Jesus' body. Something we haven't thought of."

"You mean, like he actually rose from the dead?" laughed Ken as he walked into his drive.

6

SEEING WITH FRESH EYES

"Are you coming to have a look at the back of my garden?" asked Harry. It was a week since their visit to the local. Ken was inclined to avoid referring to their conversation but had noticed a change. Harry seemed to greet him with a warmth that he hadn't felt before.

It looked as if Harry was as unfamiliar with the end of his garden as Ken was. A buddleia was standing proud, spreading its branches in all directions. Along with the sycamore tree, it had guarded the entrance to a forbidden kingdom. Behind it lay the remains of a wooden shed, the roof of which had long since collapsed, leaving a heap of planks and boards and the inevitable broken window. Weeds were well and truly in charge, and the bindweed had woven magnificent spiral patterns around the forgotten debris.

"Her next door was on at me about it when she was complaining about the tree," he explained. "She said there used to be a beautiful rockery back here, at the side of the shed. Damned if I've ever seen it!" Harry was

obviously sceptical about its existence. Ken had to admit that, at first sight, he couldn't see anything to back up what Florence had said.

Then something caught Ken's eye. He noticed the way the ground was banked towards the back of the garden. He pulled away some tufts of grass and gasped with surprise as two white decorative stones came into view. "Harry! Go and get a fork. We've got to have a look at this!" Sure enough, it wasn't long before a whole row of stones began to stand out, with a gap in the middle where two steps had been created.

Ken couldn't stop himself remarking, "It's just like when you told me God never does anything, Harry. You begin to see what he does when you start to look for it!"

"What, you mean a load of coincidences?" retorted Harry. But Ken didn't answer back. He was exploring just like a small boy in a rock pool, carefully picking his way between the weeds with his hands.

"Look! You've two little campanulas, a patch of primula, bluebells, sedum, mossy saxifrage, an alpine potentilla... Harry, it's not that you *had* a rockery. You've still got one! Florence was right after all."

Harry coughed.

"It's like what happens when you live each day with Jesus," enthused Ken. "One day it's some lost keys found. A vital document turning up. A word of encouragement that a friend says hit just the right spot. Another day, a sum of money arriving that exactly meets a need. A prayer for a friend's nosebleed to stop so he can play in a concert. A worship time at church where the music makes you feel you're in heaven. You can dismiss them all individually, but taken together they make a rockery of answered prayer.

"And sometimes, just occasionally, something big happens that's very hard to dismiss. Our vicar knows someone who damaged his leg in a car accident. He was in hospital where the doctors were considering amputating it. The church leaders prayed for him and anointed him with oil. When the surgeon who first saw him came to inspect the leg, he thought they must have swapped patients. And two weeks later he was out and about, walking normally."

Harry didn't reply, as if deep in thought. Once they reached the house, he quipped:

"Tell you what, Ken; it'll take more than a miracle to fix the bottom of my garden and get that rockery looking decent again. Why not ask your God to do that!"

Then he smiled wryly and turned to go indoors. But Ken called after him:

"No, Harry, *you* ask him!"

7

TAKING THE PLUNGE

Ken was taken aback when Harry invited him for a return visit to the pub. It was another step on the road to a deepening friendship between them as neighbours.

They talked about all sorts of 'stuff', including how Harry could plant out the fresh soil beside his rebuilt wall, how to renew his rockery, and how maybe he'd been a bit harsh on Florence. Ken made a note of this subtle change in Harry's stance.

Ken told Harry all about their bedroom window which needed replacing. He and Becky were fed up of gazing out of a misted pane of glass. Yes, a window doctor could cure that, but the window was poorly fitted and allowed a draught to blow through in cold weather. They'd had three very different quotes, all guaranteed for ten years, AA-rated. Company number one had excellent reviews. But they explained that the window would come in two parts and need jointing together. This would mean it wasn't a 'picture window'. Company number two was the cheapest; no, they wouldn't need scaffolding, and they could do it later this month. But their reviews on the internet suggested that whilst their product was good, their administration was shambolic. Company number three seemed reliable, traditional and had good reviews but didn't offer an imaginative design.

Becky had done her homework, asked all her friends, but still there was no clear winner. They were both getting frustrated and were chasing each other's arguments round in circles.

As Ken returned to the table after buying his round, Harry asked, "…er, y'know, Ken, how did you and Becky… erm… sort of… get religious? Were your parents like that?"

Ken explained that it all began when their daughter Sally had a cancer scare, through the kindness of a Christian doctor and the courage of another patient, Miriam, at the hospital where she was being treated. "It made us ask some big questions about where our lives were going. Miriam had to have a full mastectomy, and yes, it upset her, but she wasn't afraid of dying. Her eyes shone, and it had a big impact on us all." And Ken told Harry all about their journey to faith.

"Thing is, Ken," asked Harry, "I'm bothered 'cause there are so many different religions; how d'you know yours is the right one?"

"I find it hard to answer that," replied Ken, "because I've only experienced one of them. But you could have asked yourself why you accepted Jack's offer when there were several other tree surgeons in town. You didn't look into them all, did you? You took a golden opportunity when it came, and I think that's what we did when we had the chance to follow Jesus. It didn't occur to us to do a study of world religions!"

"Okay then, here's my other biggie. The folks who come to this pub all say religion causes more wars than everything else put together. It's why all these extremists plant bombs. What d'you say to that?"

"Here's one for my vicar, I think!" answered Ken. "All I can say is that Becky and I follow Jesus, and it's brought us the most wonderful peace in our own lives, in our marriage; it's helping to heal a family rift, and I'm becoming much more of a peacemaker at work. We can't avoid conflict, neither could Jesus, but he made it quite clear he wasn't interested in taking up arms. I can find out more if you like – but any more biggies, Harry?"

Harry grinned but said nothing.

Ten minutes later, as they left to walk home, Ken said, "Harry, there are times when you have to go with your 'gut' and take the plunge. Becky and I won't get a definite answer about who's the best window company for us. And you'll never find all the answers to your questions about faith. Let's see who wins. Will you

decide to become a Christian first, or will we sign a contract for our window?"

Harry smiled, and playfully punched Ken's arm.

8

TERMS AND CONDITIONS

"I'm right proud of him!" exclaimed Harry, as he stood on Ken and Becky's patio bathing in the pleasure of his son Billy's good news. "Landed the manager's job at the age of thirty-two, and he deserves it after all that hard work."

Billy had started work as an apprentice mechanic at a national motor dealership after leaving school. He'd worked his way through college to achieve his NVQ and diplomas, but had honed his skills by taking a job working 'at the sharp end' at a family firm. He soon proved indispensable, showing a talent for dealing with customers.

Earlier this year, the ageing owner Wilf had decided to let his son run the business, but to everyone's surprise he'd declined. So, they turned to Billy, who had just said yes.

"But he didn't just accept it straightaway," explained Harry. "With two young'uns, he wanted to make sure he wasn't working all the hours God sends like old Wilf did. He wanted his holidays too. And a bonus for if he's successful. And they agreed some terms and conditions they were all happy with."

Ken and Becky smiled, pleased to see Harry so cheerful.

"Now then, I've summat to ask you," ventured Harry. Aware of her list of jobs, and Harry's questions which took a while to answer, Becky left the two men to talk and went indoors. "If I'm going to do like you and believe in Jesus, what sort of terms and conditions do I get? I mean, if I go to the trouble of following him, what do I get in return?"

"Well, first of all," replied Ken, "let's ask what your part would be. Following Jesus means learning to communicate with him. I set aside half an hour every day. I read and ponder on a short passage from the Bible, 'cause this helps me understand how God thinks. I talk to him; in other words, I pray. And I listen in silence because often God drops thoughts into my head.

"Then, following Jesus means being part of his family. We don't so much 'go to' church, we 'belong to' church. We show God how much we appreciate him; in other words, we worship. We listen to teaching, study together, pray together. We care for each other. We have fun together, plan together and we organise. And then we bring other people to share what we have. Oh, and I mustn't forget – we give generously!"

At this point, Ken noticed Harry squirm.

"So, what would you get for that? You'd have a new start, feel forgiven, be free to overcome destructive habits. You'd be able to forgive past hurts and be free of regrets. You'd feel loved and affirmed. You'd be surprised to find you had personality gifts you never knew about. God has a way of putting us to work, and you'd feel useful. You'd make new friends, all ages…"

"Hold on, Ken!" said Becky, who'd just appeared to collect some dirty mugs. "It sounds like you're talking about terms of employment with God! That isn't how I see it…"

"Aw, c'mon Becks!" protested Ken. "You know I don't mean it like that!"

"When I first asked Jesus to come into my life," said Becky, "I didn't offer anything to God. I couldn't. I was so aware that I was dirty inside. I'd understood how Jesus died such a horrible, cruel death so I could be made clean. How much he and God loved me, just as I am. All I could do was to throw myself into his arms and say, 'Here's my life. Make of it whatever you can.' There was no negotiating. He's God, and I couldn't make conditions of my own."

Neither Harry nor Ken spoke another word.

9

A GLIMPSE OF ETERNITY

"Any chance I could come with you?" asked Harry. Ken and Becky winked at each other.

Florence had been fortunate in that her daily care visitor had arrived shortly after her stroke two days ago. The carer had summoned an ambulance straightaway, so that the hospital could treat her in time to avoid serious brain damage. Ken and Becky were going to visit that afternoon.

As a hobby, Becky enjoyed needlework and had a drawer full of framed flower pictures. It was easy to choose one for Florence. What would Harry bring as a gift? As they got into the car, he produced a small parcel. "Wait and see what I'm giving her!" he said.

Ken and Becky went in first. Poor Florence couldn't communicate, so they cheerfully shared their recent family news including showing photos of their Welsh holiday. They were sure Florence smiled when they told her about the baby's antics, especially the day she knocked her potty all over the floor. They finished by

gently placing their hands on her shoulder and praying for her.

Then Becky let Harry take her place. Harry was visibly shaken as he saw Florence so helpless, so frail and unable to speak. But he held his nerve. "Hello Florence, I thought you'd like to see what Ken and I found at the bottom of my garden," he said.

Ken opened his phone and shared a few pictures of the secret rockery that Florence had insisted was there.

"So, you were right!" Harry continued. "Oh, and I've brought you a little something to help you get better. I found it in a drawer at home. I hope you like it."

To Ken's amazement, Harry unwrapped his parcel to reveal an elegant cross on a necklace. Ken didn't believe in charms, but it seemed Harry now recognised that the cross of Jesus had real power. Florence couldn't say 'thank you', but it was moving to see the two of them hold eye contact in a way that expressed sympathy and appreciation, something that would never have happened until recently.

On the journey home, Harry said, "Wow, wasn't that scary? Hasn't Florence had a close call! It could have been me, couldn't it? I used to be a chain smoker and I still have the odd cig. And I know I've got high blood pressure."

"It could have been any of us, Harry," replied Becky. "Yes, it's scary, but Ken and I are prepared for whatever happens, so we don't have to be afraid of dying."

"Oh! I forgot that yesterday, when we were talking about the benefits of being Christians," said Ken. "We're looking forward to heaven and we begin to experience it here on earth."

Back home, they invited Harry in for tea and a scone. For five minutes Harry ate and sipped in silence. Then he said:

"I think it's time for me to do what you did back when your Sally had her cancer scare. I'm ready to start. I want what you've got and I want to go to heaven. With no terms or conditions!"

"Harry, that's fantastic!" chorused Ken and Becky. "Shall we pray?"

That afternoon, Harry told Jesus that he wanted to make a new start. He was sorry he'd lived just to please himself, and now he wanted to accept God's free gift. He thanked Jesus for dying on the cross so he could be forgiven and become clean inside. From now on, he'd live to please God, to come to know him and to be a part of his 'team'. He was looking forward to having a new adventure and living with Jesus as his companion. All with no terms or conditions.

THE END

Thank you for reading *Over the Garden Wall*. Would you now like to read *Why Jesus?* If whoever gave you this book doesn't have one, it's available from most Christian bookshops and from many church bookstalls. Or, you may prefer to buy from the Eden online bookshop: *www.eden.co.uk/why-jesus*

If all else fails, or even if it doesn't but you'd like to tell me what you thought of this booklet, please email me (john_hearson@yahoo.co.uk) and I'll post you a *Why Jesus?* at cost price plus P&P. I'd love to hear from you!

– John –